Y0-EBA-833

A Special Gift

For: Renee

From: Dick & Margaret

Date: 8/15/03
"moving in day"

Copyright © 2001

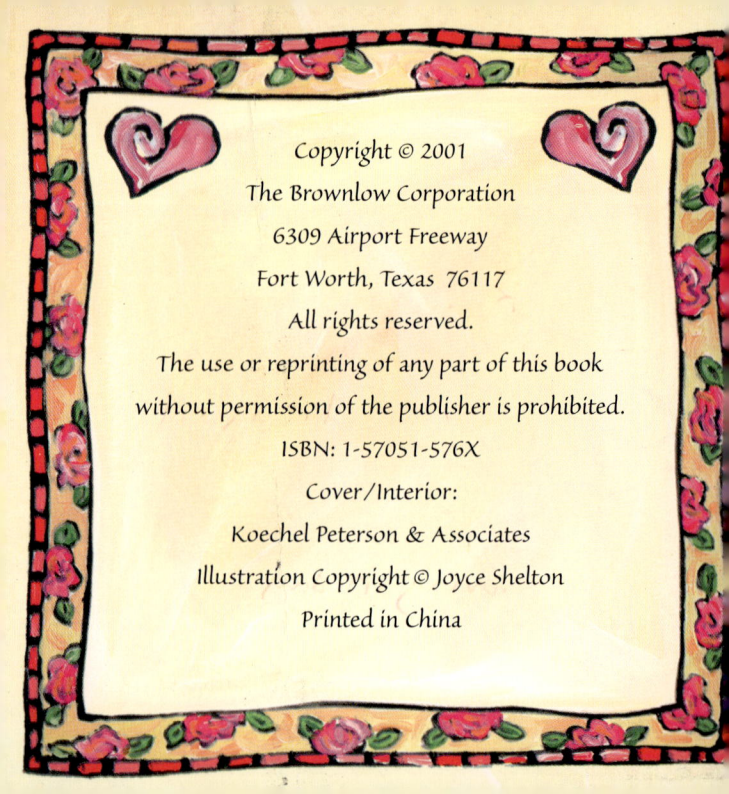

The Brownlow Corporation

6309 Airport Freeway

Fort Worth, Texas 76117

All rights reserved.

The use or reprinting of any part of this book

without permission of the publisher is prohibited.

ISBN: 1-57051-576X

Cover/Interior:

Koechel Peterson & Associates

Illustration Copyright © Joyce Shelton

Printed in China

Love & Friendship

Little Treasures Miniature Books

75 Ways to Spoil Your Grandchild
A Little Book of Love
A Little Book for Tea Lovers
A Little Book of Blessings
A Roof With a View
Baby's First Little Book
Baby Oh Baby ♥ Catch of the Day
Dear Daughter ♥ Dear Teacher
For My Secret Pal ♥ Friends

Grandmother
Happiness Is Homemade
Happy Birthday
How Does Your Garden Grow?
Little Leaves of Gold for Daughters
Little Leaves of Gold for Friends
Little Leaves of Gold for Moms
Little Leaves of Gold for Sisters
Love & Friendship
Mom ♥ Sisters
Tea Time Friends
They Call It Golf

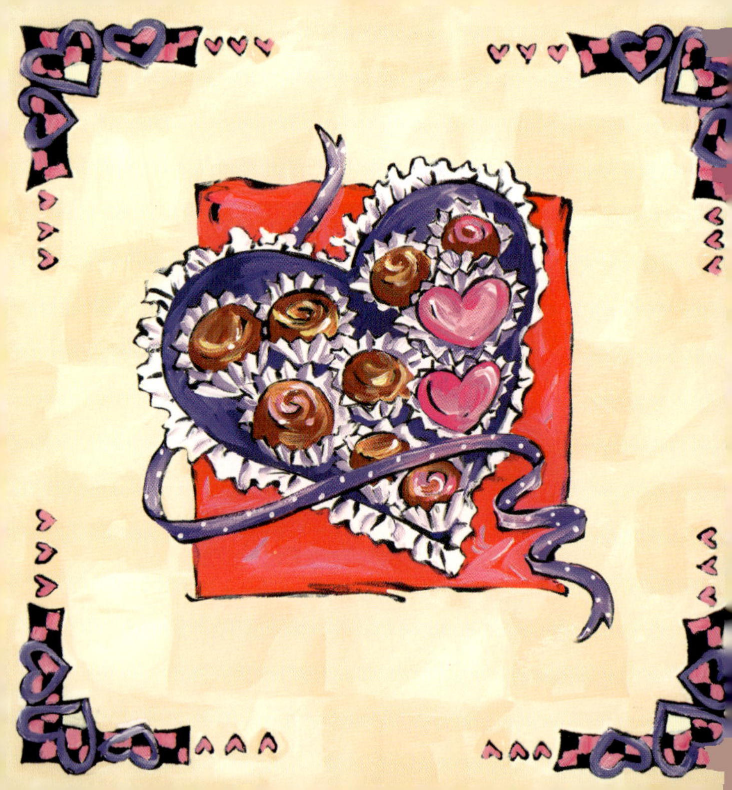

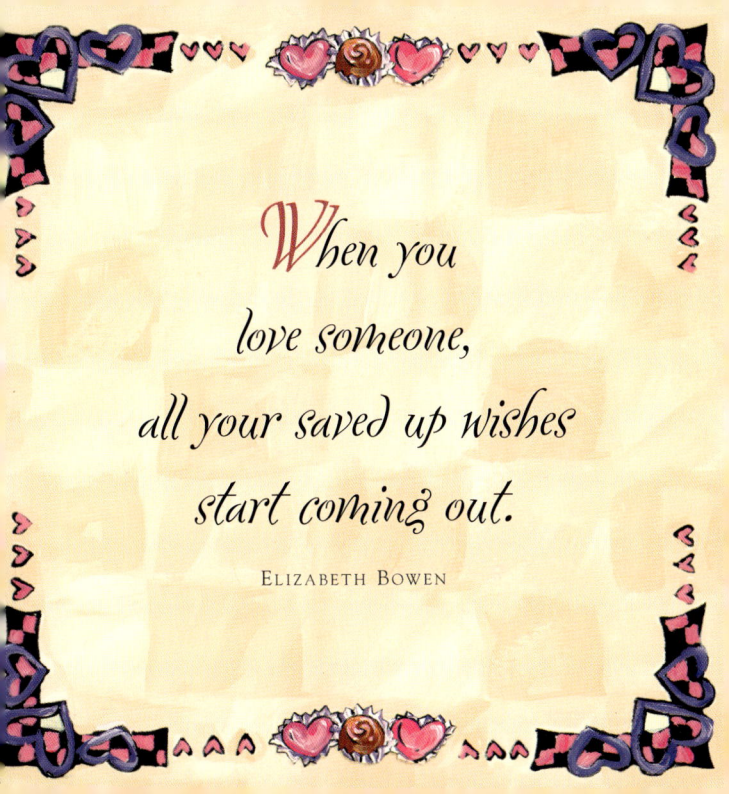

When you love someone, all your saved up wishes start coming out.

ELIZABETH BOWEN

Love doesn't make the world go round.
Love is what makes the ride worthwhile.

F.P. JONES

God loves each of us as if there
were only one of us.

ST. AUGUSTINE

Those who bring sunshine to the lives of
others cannot keep it from themselves.

SIR JAMES M. BARRIE

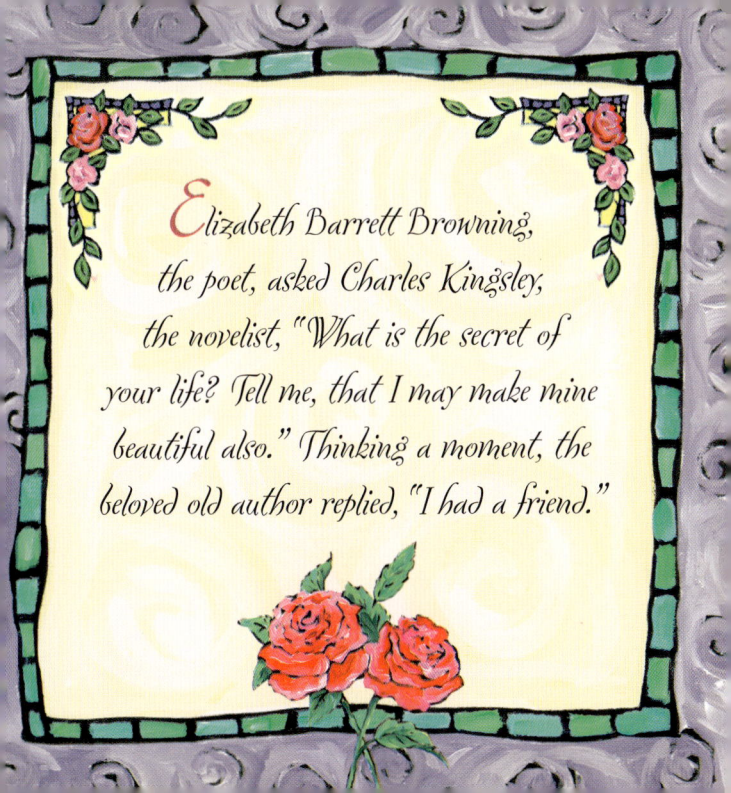

Elizabeth Barrett Browning, the poet, asked Charles Kingsley, the novelist, "What is the secret of your life? Tell me, that I may make mine beautiful also." Thinking a moment, the beloved old author replied, "I had a friend."

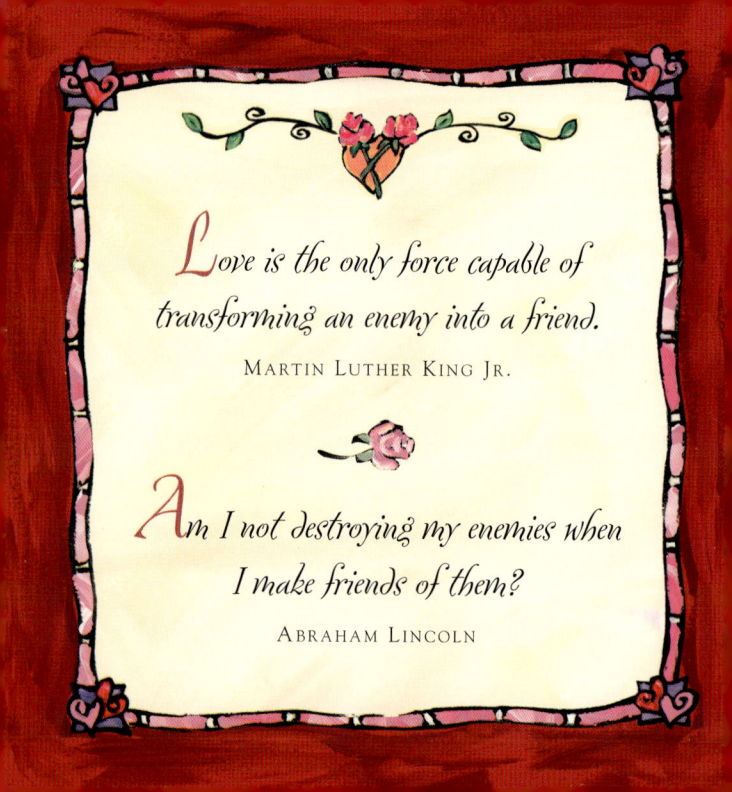

Love is the only force capable of transforming an enemy into a friend.

MARTIN LUTHER KING JR.

Am I not destroying my enemies when I make friends of them?

ABRAHAM LINCOLN

The only way to have a friend is to be one.

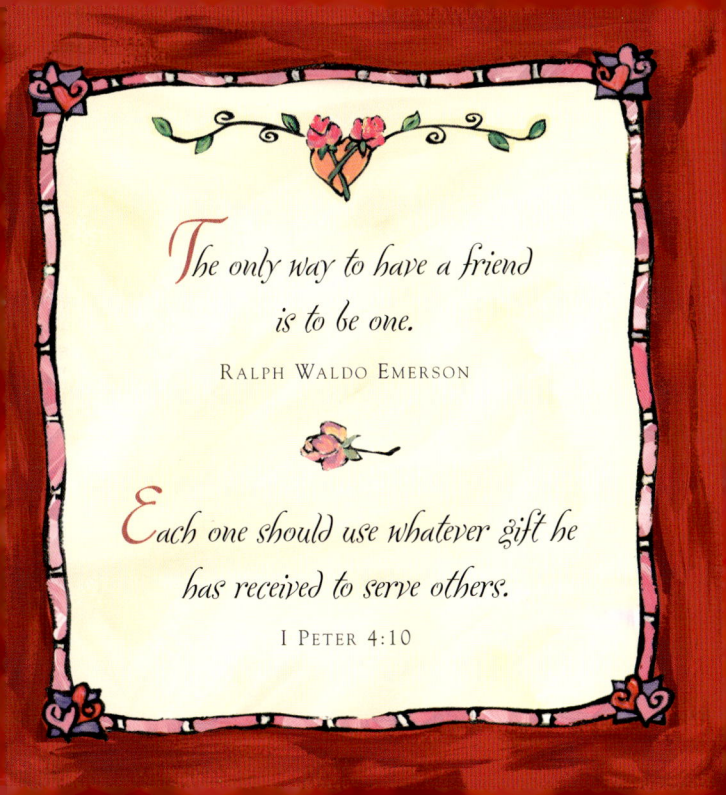

RALPH WALDO EMERSON

Each one should use whatever gift he has received to serve others.

I PETER 4:10

If I can stop one heart from breaking,
I shall not live in vain;
If I can ease one life the aching,
Or cool one pain,
Or help one lonely person
into happiness again,
I shall not live in vain.

EMILY DICKINSON

Keep your face to the sunshine and you cannot see the shadows.

HELEN KELLER

Friendship is one of the sweetest joys of life. Many might have failed beneath the bitterness of their trial had they not found a friend.

CHARLES HADDON SPURGEON

A true friend loves at all times.

PROVERBS 17:17

*I think true love is never blind,
But rather brings an added light,
An inner vision quick to find
The beauties hid from common sight.*

PHOEBE CARY

A true friend is someone who thinks that you are a good egg even though she knows that you are slightly cracked.

B. MELTZER

While faith makes all things possible, it is love that makes all things easy.

GERARD MANLEY HOPKINS

It probably would be all right if we'd love our neighbors as we love ourselves, but could they stand that much affection?

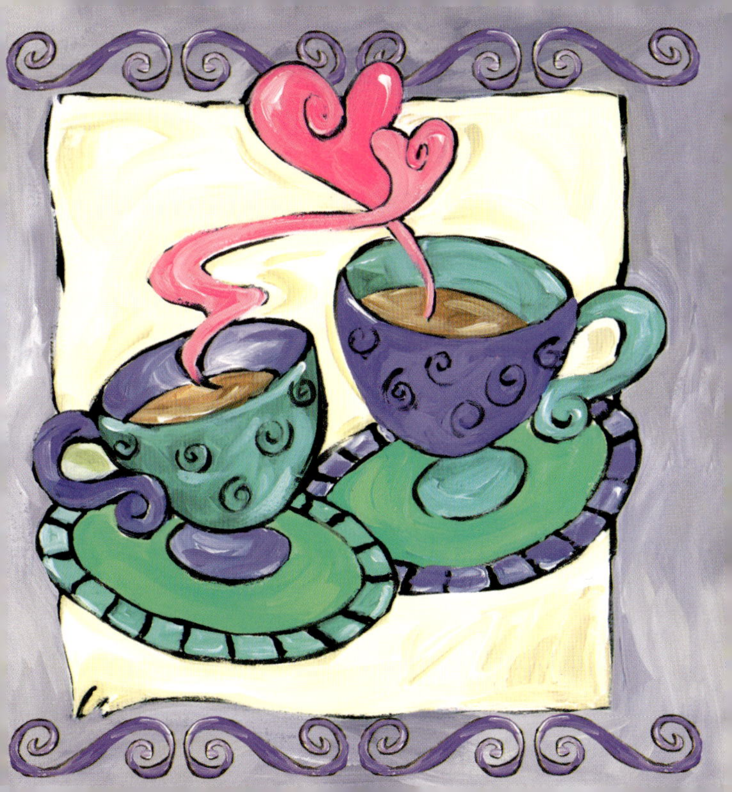

The widest thing in the universe is not space; it is the potential capacity of the human heart.

A. W. TOZER

*God knows, He loves, he cares,
Nothing His truth can dim;
He gives His very best to those
Who leave the choice to Him.*

They are rich who have friends.

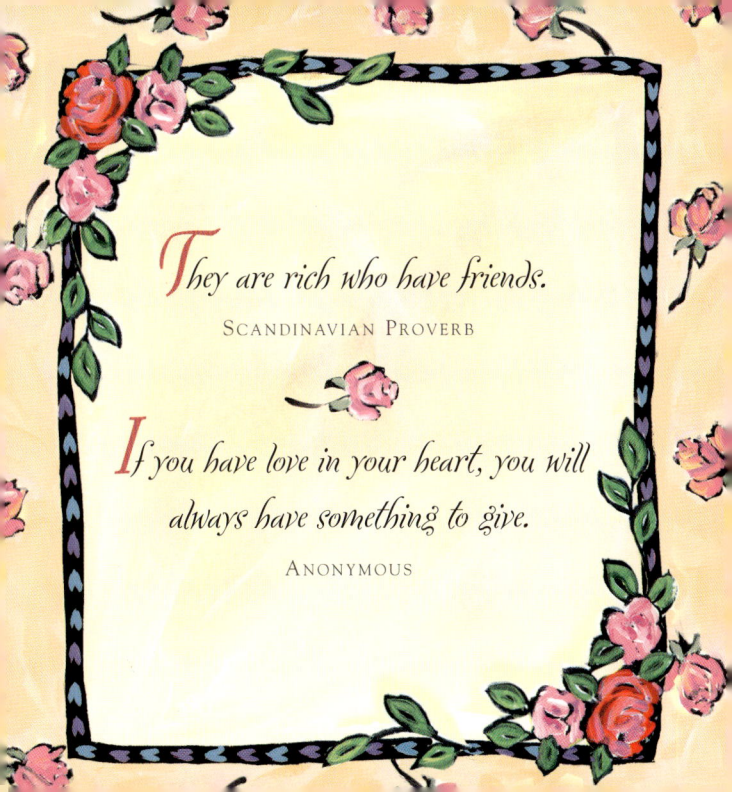

SCANDINAVIAN PROVERB

If you have love in your heart, you will always have something to give.

ANONYMOUS

And love in the heart wasn't put there to stay; Love isn't love 'til you give it away.

OSCAR HAMMERSTEIN II

Live well. Laugh often. Love much.

Love comforteth like sunshine after rain.

WILLIAM SHAKESPEARE

If I had a single flower for every time I think about you, I could walk forever in my garden.

CLAUDIA GRANDI

Love is the poetry of the senses.

HONORE DE BALZAC

Your friend is the person who knows all about you, and still likes you.

ELBERT HUBBARD

A friend is someone who listens with the heart.

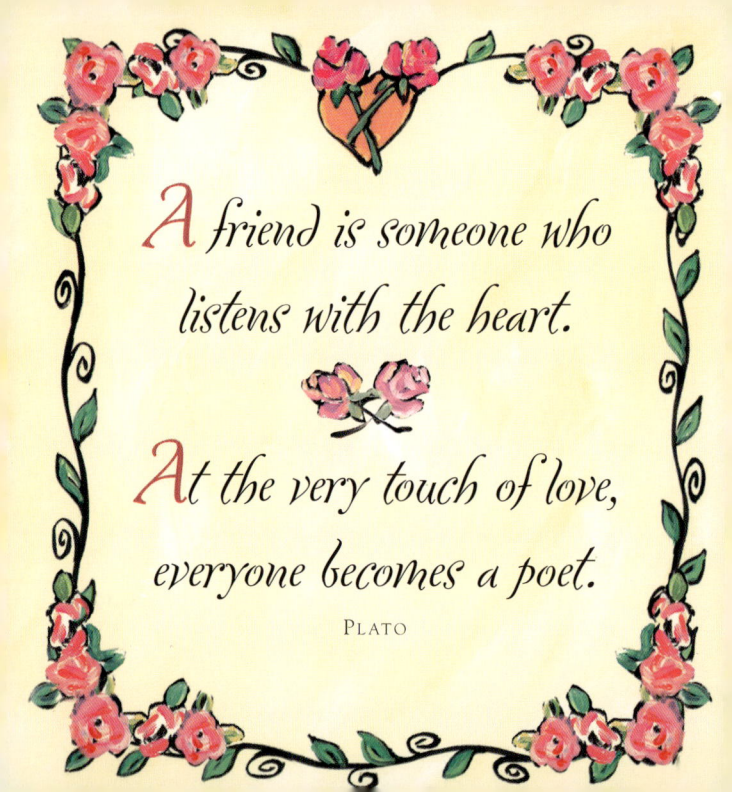

At the very touch of love, everyone becomes a poet.

PLATO

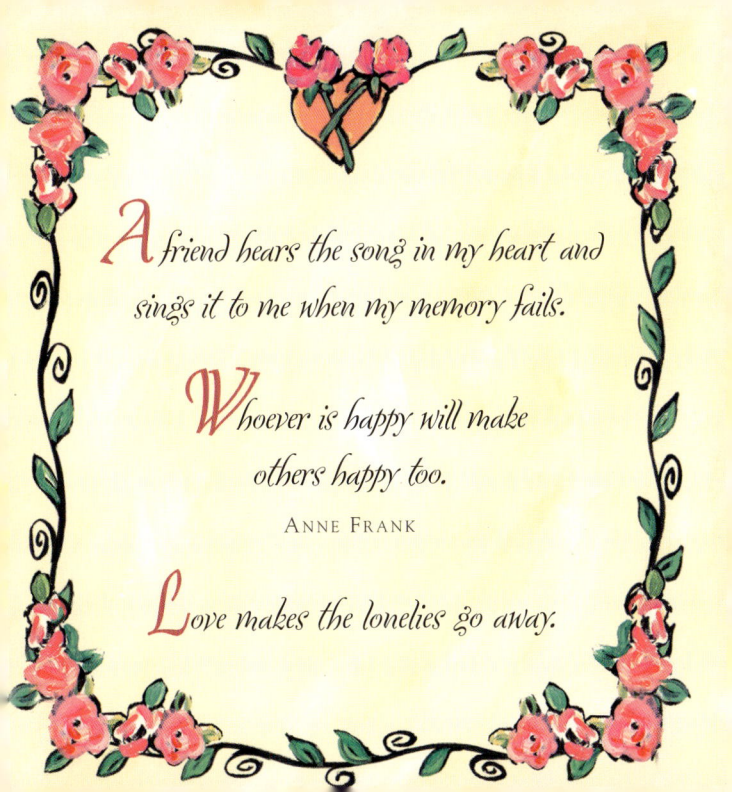

A friend hears the song in my heart and sings it to me when my memory fails.

Whoever is happy will make others happy too.

ANNE FRANK

Love makes the lonelies go away.

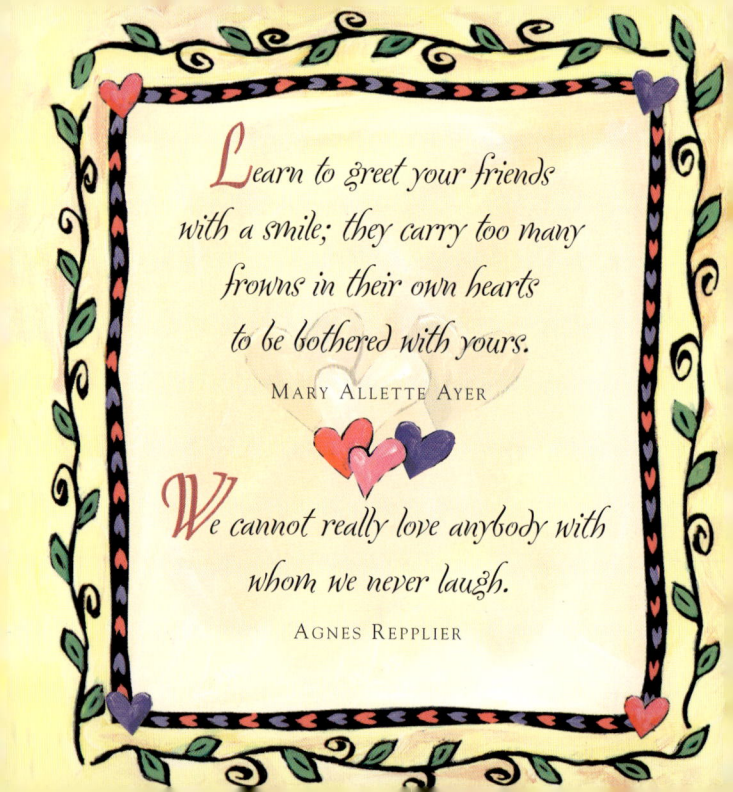

Learn to greet your friends with a smile; they carry too many frowns in their own hearts to be bothered with yours.

MARY ALLETTE AYER

We cannot really love anybody with whom we never laugh.

AGNES REPPLIER

What is the opposite of two?
A lonely me, a lonely you.

RICHARD WILBUR

Friendship makes daylight in the understanding, out of darkness and confusion of thought.

FRANCIS BACON

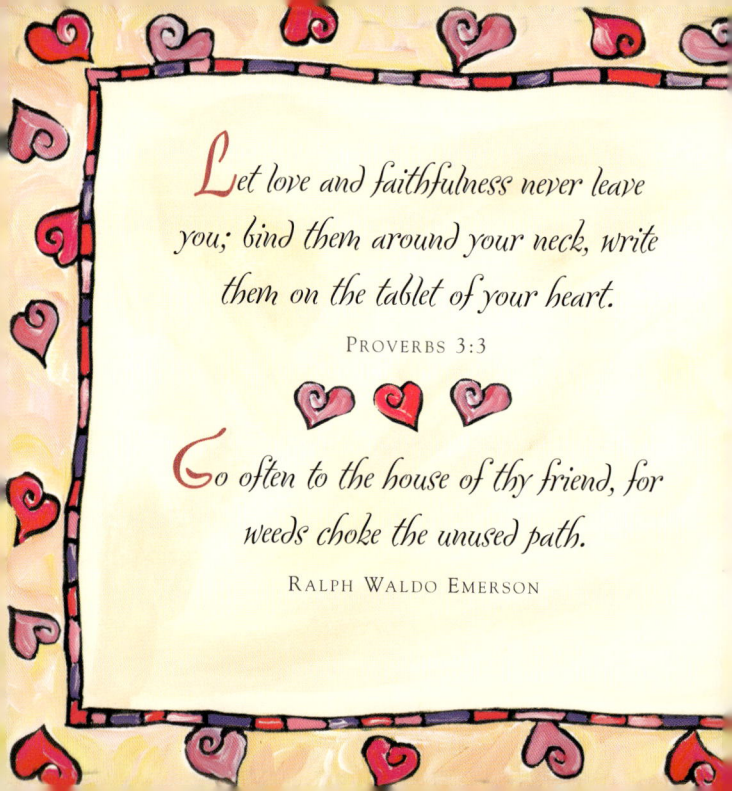

Let love and faithfulness never leave you; bind them around your neck, write them on the tablet of your heart.

PROVERBS 3:3

Go often to the house of thy friend, for weeds choke the unused path.

RALPH WALDO EMERSON

Friends

Fill their lives with sweetness. Speak approving, cheering words while their ears can hear them, and while their hearts can be thrilled and made happier. The kind things you mean to say when they are gone, say before they go.

GEORGE W. CHILDS

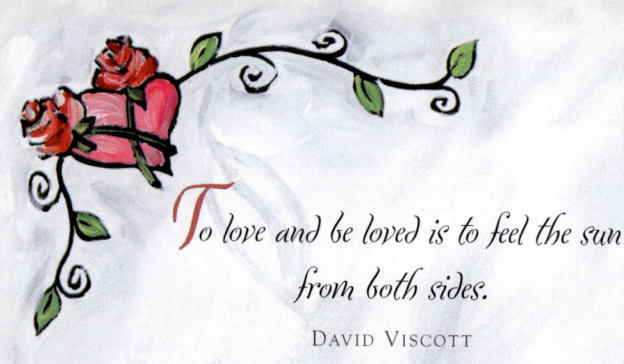

To love and be loved is to feel the sun from both sides.

DAVID VISCOTT

Happiness depends on what happens; joy does not.

OSWALD CHAMBERS

Two are better than one, because they have a good return for their work: If one falls down, his friend can help him up.

ECCLESIASTES 4:9,10

God has not promised
Skies always blue...
Flower strewn pathways
All our lives through.

God has not promised
Sun without rain...
Joy without sorrow,
Peace without pain.

But God has promised
Strength for the day…
Rest for the laborer,
Light for the way.
Grace for the trials,
Help from above…
Unfailing sympathy,
Undying love.

ANNIE JOHNSON FLINT

I'd Like to Be

I'd like to be the sort of friend that you have been to me. I'd like to be the help that you've always been glad to be. I'd like to mean as much to you each minute of the day as you have meant old friend of mine, to me along the way.

EDGAR A. GUEST

The heart is happiest when
it beats for others.

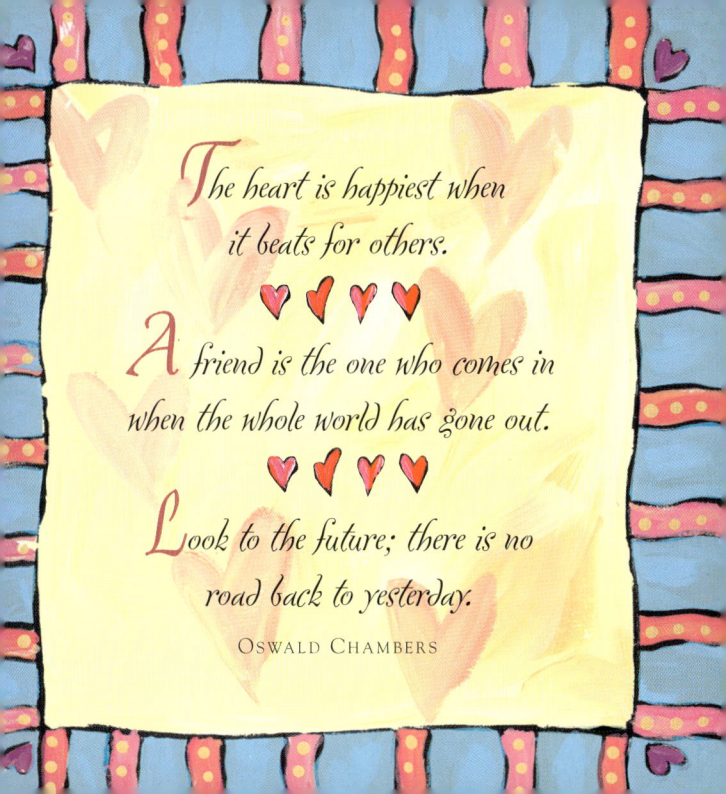

♥ ♥ ♥ ♥

A friend is the one who comes in
when the whole world has gone out.

♥ ♥ ♥

Look to the future; there is no
road back to yesterday.

OSWALD CHAMBERS

Someday

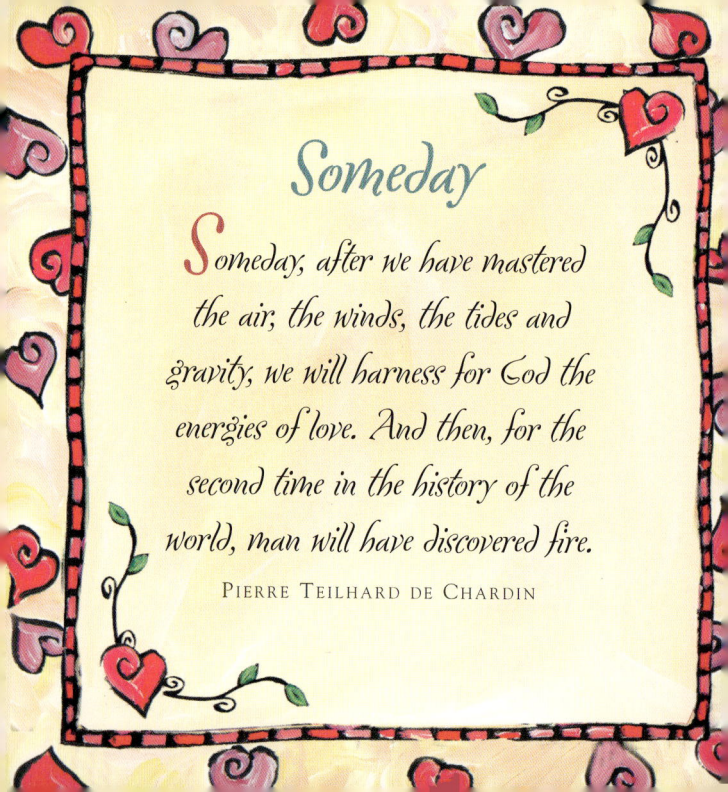

Someday, after we have mastered the air, the winds, the tides and gravity, we will harness for God the energies of love. And then, for the second time in the history of the world, man will have discovered fire.

PIERRE TEILHARD DE CHARDIN

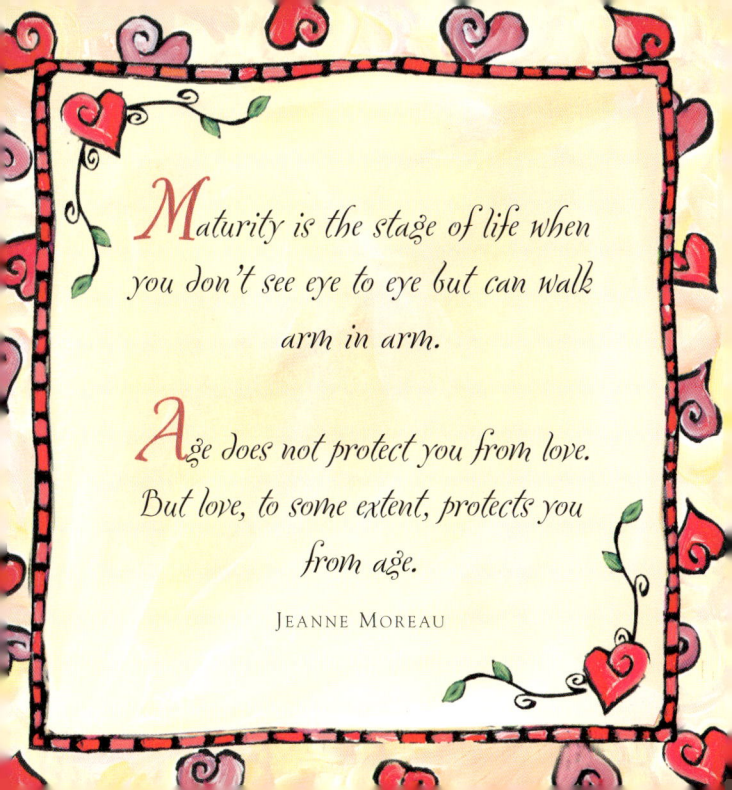

Maturity is the stage of life when you don't see eye to eye but can walk arm in arm.

Age does not protect you from love. But love, to some extent, protects you from age.

JEANNE MOREAU

Your love has given me great joy.

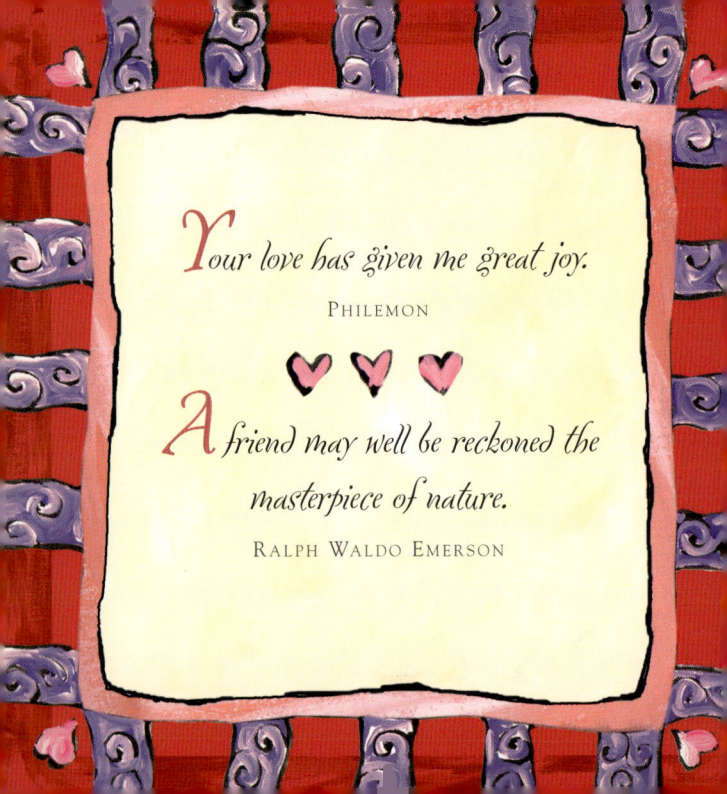

PHILEMON

A friend may well be reckoned the masterpiece of nature.

RALPH WALDO EMERSON

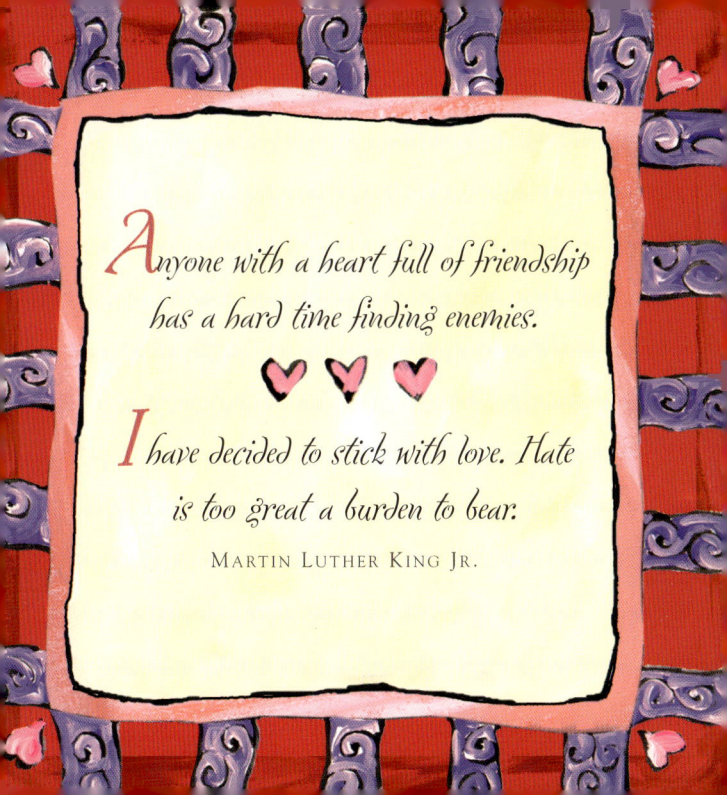

Anyone with a heart full of friendship has a hard time finding enemies.

♥ ♥ ♥

I have decided to stick with love. Hate is too great a burden to bear.

MARTIN LUTHER KING JR.

Be completely humble and gentle; be patient, bearing with one another in love.

EPHESIANS 4:2

*Love has no thought of self!
Love sacrifices all things
to bless the thing it loves.*

LORD LYTTON

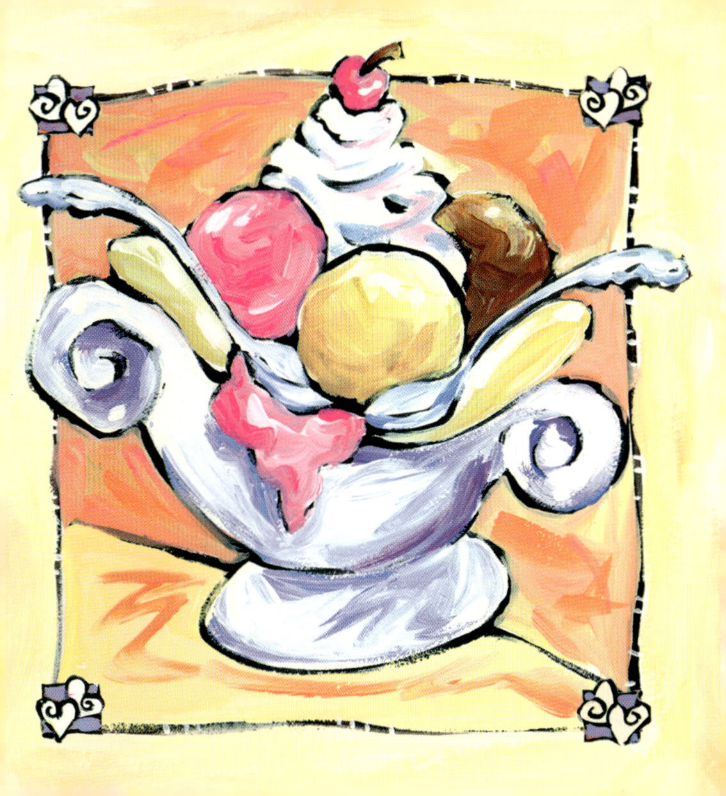

Without love and kindness, life is cold, selfish, and uninteresting, and leads to distaste for everything. With kindness, the difficult becomes easy, the obscure clear; life assumes a charm and its miseries are softened. If we knew the power of kindness, we should transform this world into a paradise.

CHARLES WAGNER

Real friends have a great time doing absolutely nothing together.

ANONYMOUS

We are all born for love. It is the principle of existence and its only end.

BENJAMIN DISRAELI

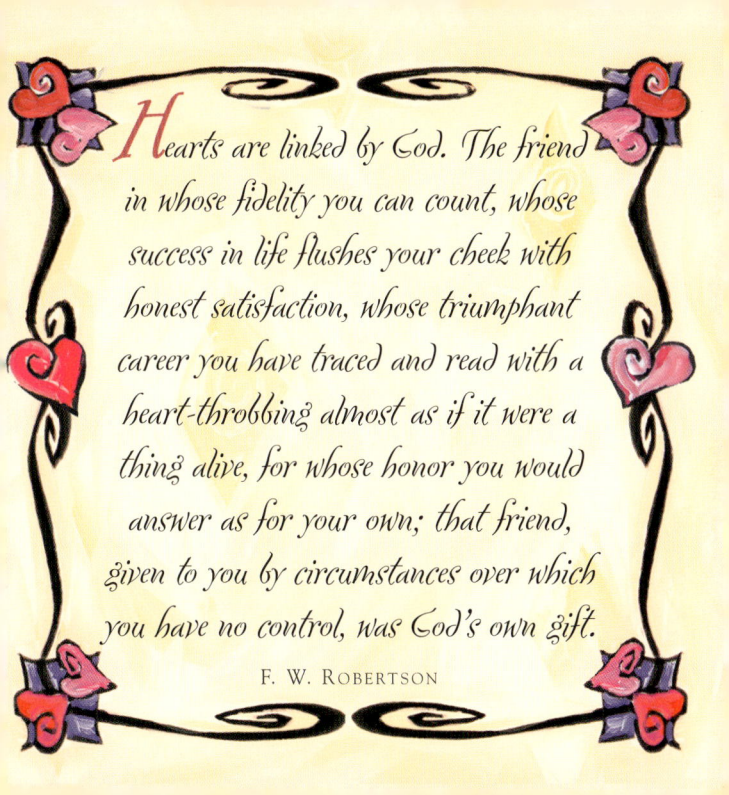

Hearts are linked by God. The friend in whose fidelity you can count, whose success in life flushes your cheek with honest satisfaction, whose triumphant career you have traced and read with a heart-throbbing almost as if it were a thing alive, for whose honor you would answer as for your own; that friend, given to you by circumstances over which you have no control, was God's own gift.

F. W. ROBERTSON

Amazing Baloney

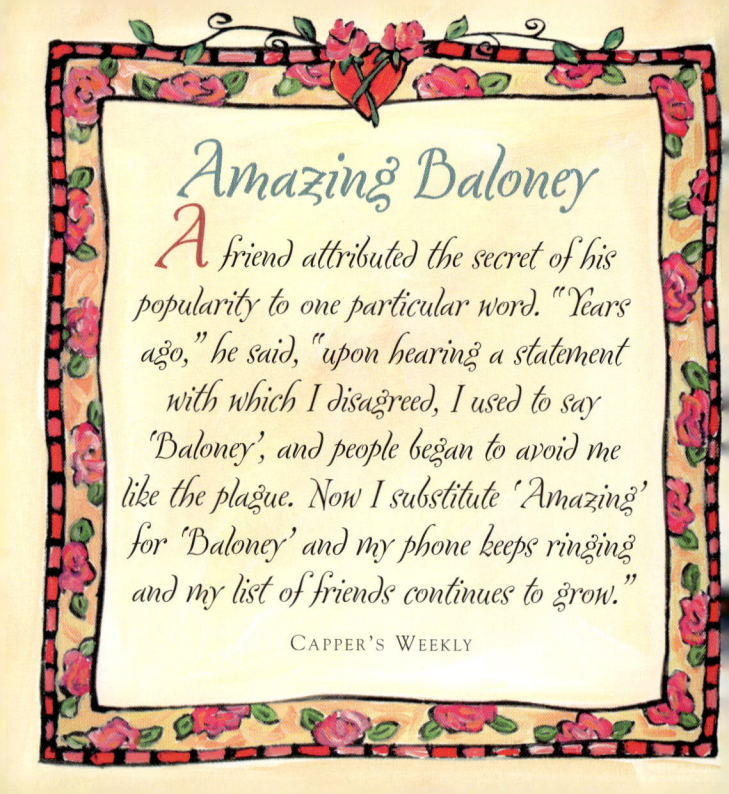

A friend attributed the secret of his popularity to one particular word. "Years ago," he said, "upon hearing a statement with which I disagreed, I used to say 'Baloney', and people began to avoid me like the plague. Now I substitute 'Amazing' for 'Baloney' and my phone keeps ringing and my list of friends continues to grow."

CAPPER'S WEEKLY

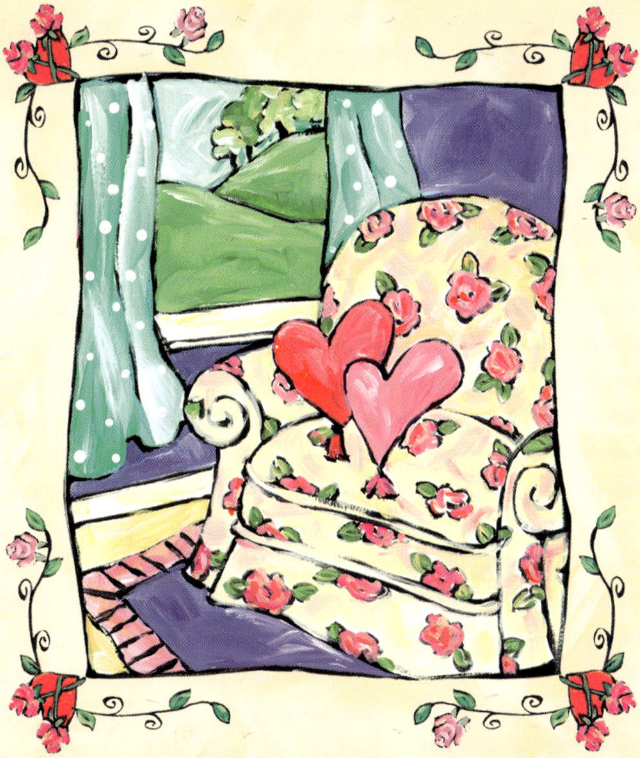

The love we give away is the only love we keep.

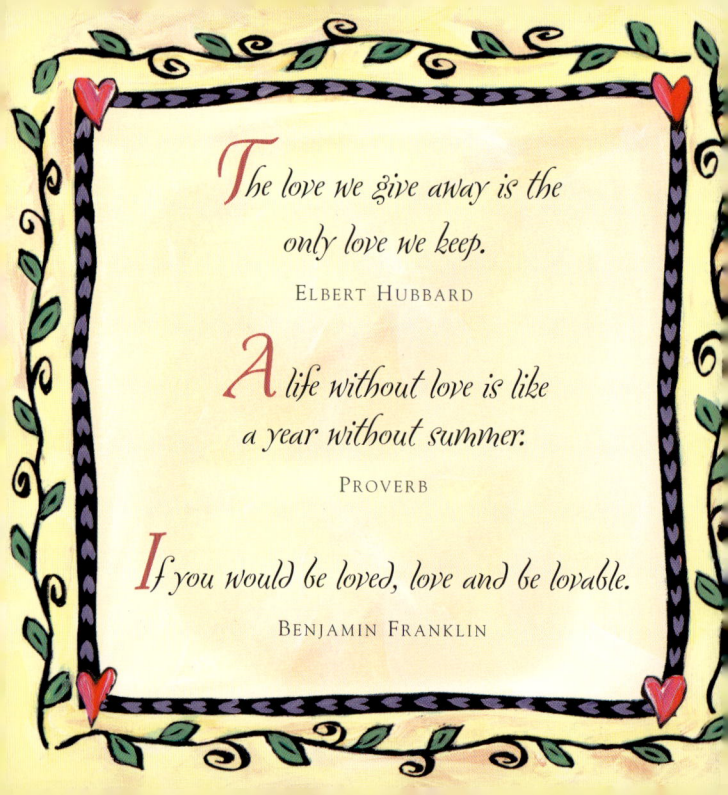

ELBERT HUBBARD

A life without love is like a year without summer.

PROVERB

If you would be loved, love and be lovable.

BENJAMIN FRANKLIN

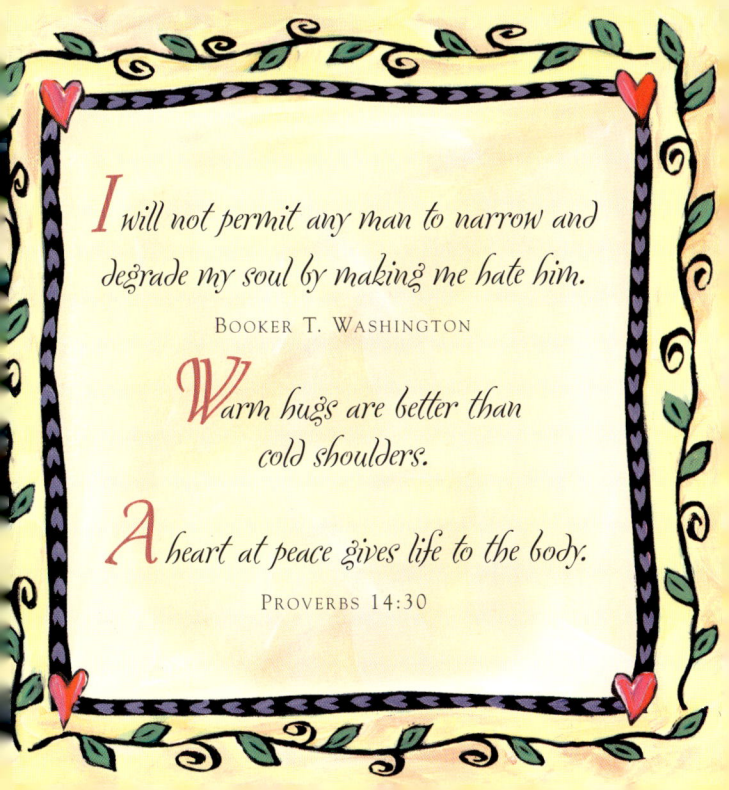

I will not permit any man to narrow and degrade my soul by making me hate him.

BOOKER T. WASHINGTON

Warm hugs are better than cold shoulders.

A heart at peace gives life to the body.

PROVERBS 14:30

There are two ways to live your life. One is as though nothing is a miracle. The other is as though everything is a miracle.

ALBERT EINSTEIN